MIRRO

CW01622499

Published in 2026 by Cipher Press

203 Ryan House
12 Smeed Road
London, E3 2PE

Paperback ISBN: 978-1-917008-19-8
eBook ISBN: 978-1-917008-20-4

Copyright © Peter Scalpello 2026

The right of Peter Scalpello to be identified as the author of this work has been asserted by them in accordance with the Copyright, Designs, and Patents Act 1988.

This book is in copyright. Subject to statutory exception and to provisions of relevant collective licensing agreements, no reproduction of any part may take place without the written permission of the publisher.

This book is sold subject to the condition that it shall not, by way of trade or otherwise, be lent, re-sold, hired out, or otherwise circulated without the publisher's prior consent in any form of binding or cover other than that which it is published and without a similar condition including this condition being imposed on the subsequent purchaser.

Printed and bound in the UK by TJ Books, Padstow, Cornwall

Distributed by Turnaround Publisher Services

Cover Design by Wolf

Typeset by Laura Jones-Rivera / lauraflojo.com

www.cipherpress.co.uk

MIRRORSTAGE

PETER SCALPELLO

Cipher
press

for us

If we know where we are when we turn this way or that way, then we are orientated

Sara Ahmed

And that is what I am saying about lying: it can give one a much better high than fiction

Renee Gladman

PROLOGUE

BENT

LONERS

EDGE

EPILOGUE

OH, EMPTINESS

there's a sort of emptiness . . .
I don't know what it is
Sharon Olds

The next thing, a murmuration of pigeons above
the dull train platform reveals groupthink, and
shapeshifts. I keep my eye on the outlier, soaring
into whichever direction they feel.

A large sash window faces the clients'
chair at the office I share with a colleague. Scurrying in
this morning I found it had been left open overnight,
and three of the birds taken relief about the carpet.
Their occupation seemed to mimic the therapy
room itself, an improvised respite and infiltration.
Once the pane was lifted enough, they shooed on.

I recognised a need for vanishing.

A certain type of full-length mirror is called a psyche
T Fleischmann

I imagine the insides of myself sometimes—
part female, part male, part terrible dragon
Ada Limón

tell a story

it's about to rain

PROLOGUE STAGE

You found yourself craving narrative

I take my shame for a walk   My shame and I get on a bus

Parallel frauds puff thought into the conditional day   stoned on its light   They can't help but   light gives the iris its truest colour

They as in plural   my shame and its shelter   though both themselves are multiple   They as in the nameless *I*   a glint in silver parentheses   or outwith

My shame and I in transit receive aroused messages from a silhouette   Their username is *God*   You have the bodypart I love   so I love you   To expose one's fantasies without a known form   then   is to be divine

What of the internet is physical   has an appetite?   Its consumer
angles to read the screen in shadow
of themself   My heart   like the world   whispers on

After not long   Shame is asleep
The weather changes and sheep in the field behind stand back
up   unable to tell who started it

We move towards and away
from land on which humans needn't
interfere   wrapping tyre tracks and blood drops
'round the Earth like string   Biological anger
and the quiet violence of passivity intersect
and   meanwhile   truly I am so unappreciative
of balance

We pass alongside a town where the buildings are covered
in tarpaulin   there may have been a flood
When I started giving in
to desire   my life was washed too
Have the fish here abstained from dance?

It all rushes back to the blackened eye
Through the window I take a photograph
of what isn't mine   the image saves
A catalogue of my flesh exists in a chip
among cylindrical servers on the seabed
isn't it awful to be observed   In photos
I can see my feminine peeking through like a possibility

Recently I lay in bed for days with alcohol poisoning losing muscle softening masculinity through sickness A conversation with my immunity *I hear you I'll try harder to be real* The fictions we grant ourselves my addiction to identity

At what point does a person choose to abandon their life? Though inhabiting a finite form we are offered endless paths Have been *the...* Could be *a...* The instant a constant opportunity for juncture to be suddenly decountered Reality can be clicked together by such decisions Clicked apart

For years I have dreamt about buses frantically chasing down and missing them Checking timetables lingering through the night long after their wheels have stopped retracing the days' movements Perched under canopies of vandal-proof plastic etched with your name I wonder what latent occupation brought me here today

Back to the vehicle Shame individualised I the glowing interior shape of *self* the journey we're on towards an interesting resolution subject to hormones If memory is distance how many miles are left until the truth of my own experience?

Over the border and tones become cooler   waking up
from a vivid dream to a new   separate consciousness
Everything the same   but slightly different colours

A billboard at this point reads *www.fuckthepeople.gov.uk*
There is no person without a world   so to whom
do signs apply?   What does
mirror mean?   It means
mirror

Shame wakes   too   beside me
always after—
a sizzle of past threat   presently felt
externalising all that's traversed
as I'm persistently alive
and being dispersed   The memory
gazes-at   but Shame has

no gaze just a voice saying *It's me A man a teenager a boy a cell on the cusp of all you have ever done* And thus the entire universe is perceived solely by how humans can

I have been trying on both sides to vocalise self-unimportance yet polyphony ensues even while ignoring my navel Surely ego can only exist in relation to an interchangeable other? Shame my rank innards or inner child

I was still on the journey when I noticed I had been orientating in the wrong direction

PART ONE BENT

REFRACTAL

The ache of fathers;
            an imprinted vacancy
    in our chromosome

PSEUDOMORPH

Most caterpillars carry no trace of their past selves after molts.
Many will eat the skin they shed, swallowing a past silhouette . . .
Because molting is an act of love. It is a promise that you will grow
into yourself and your wild and unexpected future
Sabrina Imbler

The days were indigo and compressed. I puffed
grass each morning and took steady strides just
to get through them. On the marshes,
I'm transfixed by a podcast about caterpillars
in the seasonal hue of late afternoon,
which augments the silvery reeds and dew.
It's far too cold
to cruise, I can feel the contents of my bladder
refrigerating inside me. But then seeking another's warmth
would make sense. Shame is amorphous
and perpetuated by reflection, I'm inclined to look
at myself in a mirror and think *what the fuck*?
These long walks detach me from self-perception
and sense-making, the illusion of control;
to have hair and then none at all, the sink
full of it, and the bed. In four months
my eyebrows will have grown back,
restructuring my forehead.   As we age
and our barriers thin, we're dragged nevertheless
into futurity, even lying on the ground; the ice
older than our ancestors melts. Movement comes
from potential.
I ask animals how it feels to be free, and they confess
various things, mainly that they are not. Our hybrid bodies

have become drifting objects, in keeping with the mind,
a *queer form*. I too have been joyous
in the act of disappearing, a *queer future*. I wish
I could act as if I've never had a fissure; pressure
holds our flesh together, without it,
the unravelling of self.
I use my thumb to make copious notes
of little coherence, altered in language by THC
and an awe ordinarily stifled by the day-to-day.
It seems pain has nowhere to stay
when the part of you that was fractured no longer
exists. I don't even identify
as who I was yesterday.

IMODIUM

On Halloween, I ignore my guts'
survival signals in order to be social
and attend the supposedly
queer rave, which turns out to
be hundreds of men in harnesses, two
-stepping under a railway arch.
The bottle of poppers between my
genitals suggest I use my body
or let it evaporate; the fellas here
know each other on a muscular level.
A stranger who sent me photographs
of his rectum adjusts himself at the bar
beside me and we both say
nothing, clawing for attention for more
drink, for the homogenised serotonin.
The speakers blurt out *work*
work work, and occasionally I can
revel in taking orders, but
what I long for is to leave, to
suck on my lover's toe
like a vape, ride
on the stimulant of you
all weekend.

How might personal autonomy coexist with collective liberation, without obstructing the individual freedoms of others?

Whose choice
is it?

NEW OPPORTUNITIES

As I'm moved south and west through the city by libido, I reassure
myself that pleasure and survival are the drivers of all
animal behaviour.

Today I roused from a dream in which I was holding a gun
and terrified I'd turn it on someone, dreading I
could harm another with mere proximity to a
violence that was used upon then embodied by me.

Don't shoot.

Waking, I was reminded to text a friend that I hope the
workshop she attended on intergenerational trauma
was super meaningful.

Grief creates new opportunities for grief.

Is making art making a difference?

The camera obscura afforded me this gallery of dicks, sometimes
we need other witnesses than just ourselves.

I mince between internet towers, parallel selves, without
acknowledging them, pockets & pores full of
identifying information; the gooey vertebraeity of
day.

A fly-poster states *Heaven is closing* in Times New Roman, peeling
away.

I wonder how rejecting the father in reciprocity affects
one's gender role, a person being as malleable as a
word, as *protest*.

Time and again I have marched faceless on boundary street,
obscuring a genetic resemblance to my perpetrator.

The sexual organ of the brain, too, dissociates to the
embryonic pulse of transient pleasure and
survival; a body to stink and love with, despite it
all.

The past isn't-quite buried, but we must let it rot anyway, half-in
half-out of the earth, it's fertiliser.

Things can be in-between and still let go of.

A message from the clinic says *You are contagious*.

How very capable we are of leaving a mark, how cathartic.

A needle can be used to cure or to escape the need entirely.

I once was lost to drink, now losing instead to thirst.

Breed me pleads a proximate heart, and I to someone else.

Imagine the cumulative force of desire and longing felt
simultaneously across the planet, the implications
of that.

To be irreversibly altered at a molecular level with every breath: it
was poetry all along.

VIEW FROM A FEELING

Your empathy will be the death of you, the wilderness
whispers to me, but is it not mortal intuition
to recognise?
Our hearts naturally stop
between every contraction, to reflect.
In my reverted state, I'm thinking
about driving in the '90s; a quarter-century ago
reoccurs with a simple crossing
of neurones. Mum playing her soul
and country. My mother, my father
figure was her.
As an infant, I watched
her rub make-up all over her face.
I was feminised
by ruthless male incompetence
and a shared maternal body, little
breastfeeding cannibal that I was—
how *emasculating.*
We all arrive deconstructed at that age,
the stories of the places you pass through
become part of your story.
Moving yonder, too fast now
to interpret the scenery; we really can
normalise anything. The trope goes
that as a queer child, humour can
save you. As an adult, it almost can.
Humour, sexual desire, and sadness:
all the arrogance of the living, reflected
in the ignorance of my own specificity.
The search for paternal love

and the fictitious truth of memory
is a journey of losing yourself,
accompanied by shame.
Where is my paternal love? My
androgyny debt? I'm of two minds
about which
timeline I'm really
living in.

FOR THE BUZZ

I'm frottaged against recollection, retracing
the soggy streets of my teens,
as if dropped into a different decade.
Patches of green to sit and drink on,
the bridge over half of a river; the night
I sank a litre of vodka and waded into it.
It's not the place itself I experience
in returning, soberly a remarkable city,
but what went down here. The Effect of it,
its spirits to spend the hours with.
Now I'm off those tall bottles,
they didn't fix me.

A flutter among the bushes, a bird
or a bloke; that which provokes
the inner shrug. I knock about with
my ashtray heart, a power of sodomites cower
under wet canopies
for a depressed fag. I've been there,
small lakes appearing through the tarmac.
A close friend from school describes
her analogy: that in order to grow, the bereaved
must spiral outwards from their inner
bullet of grief, as it always stays the same
size inside us. Life bestows everybody
with an unnecessary burden, or maybe we all
need one—even normativity is oppressive.
We're swapping escape strategies over
her dark glass of wine, my third soft drink.
A Glaswegian odyssey. I turn into

a different person here, as selfhood only
materialises through context, hoods pulled
back up. We were absolutely out our minds,
weren't we, and the madness spilled over
into the rest of our lives.

We continue catching up, meandering
through gravestones, this haunt
for mourners where we'd blackout
into baggies, also grieving conviction
in a future. Freed by intoxicants
to be idiots for brief periods
that lasted years, feral in woods or
on a dancefloor beyond guilt, carnivorous
as we were vulnerable.

The origin of shame is in the first telling.
I watched myself gradually crawl into addiction
and, generously, let it happen. We all develop
a persona in order to survive, but you can't
muzzle adolescent feelings forever. That person
who vanishes always comes back, unwashed
and unchanged, with shame for how they move.
And it's just me, chugging away in the dark.

As the sky unloads, the land must decide how
to hold it, it often breaks its bounds to do so.
When rain subsides, terrain can eventually
absorb its downpour. This is the dance
of our relating to each other; to be *done in* here
is to be put back into oneself by violent force.
You could say that the past only exists
in the present, when it's brought to mind,
the hardened tissue of a scar describing
where you are now, not how it was created.

How strange that the days of a month, minutes
and seconds of the day repeat themselves,
yet none are ever equal.

There once was nothing to do
with the day but dream, I'd come
then lose sight of what the dream was. I wished
to be good at being a boy but was better
at being a good boy for someone else.
The chemical burn of nostrils, young lads
laughing in cars with their dads.
In showing my ACEs, pragmatism shifted
from *am I cool* to *am I coping,* and I wasn't,
so I left. Realising you no longer need
an apology can be a revelation,
the dithering shadow beside me that
resembles Shame was just my own.
After all, it's still a life.

DEEP DISH

I'm suddenly taken aback
by a particular brand of
microwaveable pizza   which unearths
a clump of memories
from my childhood

On Sundays   at his house
at the start of the century   specifically
his microwave would congeal
the cheese to glistening perfection

I realise that this
is a nice memory

That
in the years since   I hadn't
felt such a fondness   or contentment
or warmth from dwelling
on that period of my life at all

But this
recollection was just as it was   just of
the senses   and of food

A child's
microwaved pizza   and a feeling
of enjoying it somewhere difficult

OH, EMPTINESS

Round that bend there's a peripheral utopia
Kay Gabriel

Braised cattle and heavenly desserts, the future
is concrete being dug up
and rebirthed as a new wall to lean on, levels
to ascend and spend allotted heartbeats,
incomes with. This economy
of hunger. Faces I recognise
from apps but I'm not on them
right now, let the imaginary opportunity
pass. Am I some kind of maniac,
seeing sex at the World Buffet?
Or was I built simply
to observe, mere component of manoeuvres
in the sauntering of willing lives? How
easily we become naked
expressions of grief. What
freedom, to be freed from want,
a freshly constructed surface,
looking.

PART TWO LONERS

I take a cutting
of my consciousness &
let it propagate
on its own

into
poems

An evening when I'd drank too much, I ran into the road—in every moment looking for something to connect with. *And why is life worth living*? the psychiatrist later asked, testing me.

They let me out. I'm getting back on my feet, you know, getting on with things. They let me out, into the past again. We only go back because we have to. I'm on my way to tell you I'm not what you thought I was; when you're let out, you're still inside yourself.

A murmur of our deceased contemplates reformed blood flow, pharmaceutic access for the systemic depth of infection and reminiscence, as if prophylaxis were also a cure for the sea. When you first identified your reflection, what did you see? Between image and being drifts the fantasy of meaning.

My shame and I keep rolling along, heading towards a setting of prior existences. Our relation to one another and the past is like a poem, less mechanised by subject, than what it evokes. *One another and the past*—who belongs to whom?

When they let me out, I shaved my entire face and head in dysphoria, as if to erase it completely. In these moments, I am excited by lyric and the smooth resemblance of my mother; or of my father, grown to a point then cut off forever. I seek to position my self beyond a timeline of ever-resurfacing, some emerging outline, no sooner snipped away. Made of jaw and brow a nice, clean landing for a fist. Growing a beard should be easy, you just do nothing.

I recall a dyed beard who expressed intimacy with chest punching and I joined in, aggression has naturally passed for love to me. He lay on top and I enjoyed his weight, the wetness of semen connecting our hipbones, crushing me tender. Moving through water, I am often reminded of this lesser wetness, of potential I will never actualise. We compared our anti-depressants and their side effects, the variations of spit willingly entering a body. How did we reenact our childhoods then? Why do I still?

Where I grew up, there was something about maleness and being arrested, having arrests. So much of teenage masculinity was weedy thoughts and fear of getting your head kicked in, pissing by bins down lanes and trying not to look. Pissed as a thirteen-year-old and allegedly manly, I inherited the swell that dwindles; parameters of the heart exaggerated with drink, then deferred. To fuck and not be fucked, or to wish to be ruined.

God adds: I am just a hole. Right enough, we remain perpetually pubescent, still finding our form until death, which is the absence of it. To transform, you must believe in your transformation, make transformation your environment. Like the time being: revisiting places from my past to make peace with them, platonically barebacking the abyss.

Through the window, a clearing draws out clarity. Kites fly high in the gaping space, such hope in lifting and staying there. There is a grief in hope, the current lack-of. I suppose that lack can give a kind of relief. Like when I couldn't bleed enough to be tested.

On the ward one night, a few women lined up, dressed. *We're going out dancing,* they proclaimed, grins in their make-believe. A hospital is an in-between place, hole in the skin of reality. Though reality is queerer. *Don't let them tell you you're mentally ill,* one of them said to me. I thanked her. *But I am,* I thought.

The next day I painted a portrait with the art therapist of my mental state, a scab-red oval. I've grown familiar with turning the pathetic into the abstract. *It gets better,* she told me, though I swear it only gets different.

As it turns out, dependency is purely the recurrence of a need for release, a short-lived ablution. A person can clear away their body incrementally, or all at once. I yearn to feel ego leave my skeleton like a sneeze.

In one of my bus stop dreams, I'm waiting in the snow with someone I've just met. He offers a draw of his salvia joint, or I ask for some, flame slumped at its tip, knackered. And the night becomes boundless. I remember thinking life isn't so serious, I remember not a lot else, scaffolded by synthetics, the overhanging stars like synapses splitting. Both of us out on the self-destruct in guise of good times, for a lightness that turns heavy. By cringe of morning, I'd lost a kind of virginity to that blur. It wasn't even a dream.

We carry on up the road, in the midground between then and the end.

To heal through purge—vomiting, bleeding, shitting, moulting—is termed catharsis. Catharsis through excretion of the words held within you articulates itself as allegory. But life isn't scribbled like living, it's written like writing. One image gradually gives way to another, constructing a novel: fate, or autoplot. A trip is the surreal on the inside.

Why, then, should a story be more statement than question? The selectivity of memory itself provides a fictive layout. An outline of lived experience becomes the redraft of remembering, movement blearing fiction with its indentations. Literacies of living are learned from reading the signs as it goes on.

Can I narrate my life into ownership? Turning my attention to the real world, as if it were cyberspace, we pass our demolished memorials. I distract my senses back to technology, give my trauma toy a squeeze. I am, after all, writing as self-defence.

The communication of written language is an interpretation of shapes, appreciation of art. That anything can be truly defined in language is a fable, there is only honesty, expressed either earnestly or by virtue of deception. A deeper form of understanding is conceivable beyond our articulable contents—and we're supposed to take literature seriously?

How is socialism, prevention of climate catastrophe measured against the time spent phrasing this self-serving line? The blood on my hands is just below the skin, my voracious id. How can any of us live as a poet? I guess I'll keep scribbling, 'til an answer comes out.

I read on the internet that a place of repair must be distinct from that of where the damage originated, thus recovery transpires in elsewhere, enabling eventual return to the site of the wound, anew. But people say things, don't they.

In my unwell role, I was placed with my unwell peers. We established norms together, a mutual acceptance of altered states. Nobody questioned the splash of vomit dried into the wall, our faces inscrutable as stone. The nausea of survivorhood, it was practically calming.

While inside, I enter the day askew, miraculously in the present tense. In a sense, I'm freer than I've ever been, eddied along by the clinical composition of the clock; dawn landscapes witnessed through webbed windows, their own frames of tolerance. Though to exist entirely in the moment is also to live without the convenience of hindsight.

My peers carry their Shame with them too, apart from one, a gaunt son who looks as if he's had a hard time of it. Shame can be like your imaginary friend: someday you have to kill them off.

Today would be... how long since? The present is the entire afterlife of the past. This breath.

A border functions to exclude, yet a page folded in on itself repeatedly, until impossibly suppressed, still contains the cut of the whole sheet. In my reflection is your life without its corners.

The land is a living thing, often we ignore that, describe it a *disaster* when environments behave how we force them to; some gaslighting. Waves flush-towards the shore even as they recede, as with coming-of-age self-destructiveness. It soothes my inner child to receive the approval of dads, a fetish concocted of looking away from inferiority towards exaggerated paternity. Gratification can be found in the distinction between truth and just a history you've rehearsed.

Have I passed the maturation stage marked by pursuing parenthood to offset my own failed youth, or do I rather crave the radical optimism of those who choose to make a child? When I die, I will recognise the feeling. When you die, I will have already grieved.

Lots of broken glass, the pavement's answer to the canal. Where resides this density of feeling, if it holds no weight in our cells? The situation of the subject is split, it stopped adhering. I hated him. I still loved him.

It's true I opt out of existence from time to time. I've come-to in psychiatric and carceral arenas, unable to say my name, for what it's worth. In a name, you can place your whole past, an intimate history of carelessness and mundanity, and just leave it behind. Name the void you're filling, what am I called now? Point to the ghost: your mind.

There's little modesty in hospital, here I can appreciate the same is true of the world, so much taking in and shitting out. Is a wet clump of hair in the drain assigned male or female? How about a toenail, a tooth? Or when hair changes colour of its own accord? What's the gender of a protective exterior, behind which we are liquid and goo?

How do our bodies become bearable? With Shame, how was I to develop a self of my own? An example of androgynous beauty is scar tissue.

A peer says to me *We keep going, like tumbleweed, bits falling off and being added to us, until we can't keep going any longer,* sips on her vape. *After a while, you'll start moving again.*

To be misunderstood may also mean to be poetic, yet we make false connections all the time; you can feel nostalgia for an experience you didn't even enjoy, we interpret other people through our own subjectivity. I await to be diagnosed as promiscuous and let home.

I'm crooked under a white sheet, faecal stain in the shape of a smile. Life's a big laugh.

The growing threshold of pathology mirrors stages of early childhood development; when we say *our*, reaching for affinity, beside us lies a reverse route. How is a person taught to love their non-equivalent? The *I* can imitate an algebraic variable for the transposable self: an equation of emptiness could be I – I = *Y*?

Borders of body and nation—we're more expansive than that. On the waiting list of gender, my shame and I scroll through the meatland, training ourselves to open wider, cells dying and some regenerating, dodging governmental potholes.

I've removed Shame from my organs, birthed them a body of their own, yet it feels like I who occupy the wrong form. Society has made itself grandly incapable of acknowledging its true desires, so the sin of conservatism is deflected onto the queer. What is the cause of conformity? Always living in the sun, where's your shade?

Gen-der... *Gennnderrrr*. I repeat the word aloud until it sounds meaningless.

How much misery is justified and how much is illness? The ward becomes a residence of cause and effect anger and compliance A result of bodies used to regulate the compulsions of others Rising social injustice begets rising anger neglected anger begets suicidality The need to break something the object of yourself Regrettably anger gets me nowhere but closer to perpetrator If I can't be happy I'll try at least to be compliant

I have a sense here of observing significant incidents in other peoples' lives *Take your medicine feel better* Distribution as euthymia a treatment for the constructed-nonpathological But placebo bruises can't be cured by placebos

I spend most days hiding behind the door to my vague coffin of awe incapacitated and shedding myself Occasionally I stand with my arms spread as wide as they can checking my wingspan I still fall asleep in the dark thinking about verse Laid there I realised I've always been fleeing childhood male perversion and a couple more epiphanies since forgotten

It was unbearable I said to a nurse *Of course it was but you move on* she replied You move on

We travel on public transport
as if everything were normal
in our lives   on our way
to make a living   or escape
People searching
for necessity and the means
with which to earn it   Everybody exhausted
On a bus I can be heartbroken
privately   pushed along thoroughfares
like peristalsis   With the ride
I sense the shape of relapse and direct it
off-centre   my reactionary
regionality   At times we long to be
run over by the vessel while we're
still inside it

We pass through suburbs   lines
of noses on the edge
of a pool table   to the outskirts
of town   factories
producing painkillers   making record
profits   abandoned units
where kids take lunch-money spirits
and husbands their skeletons   men
operating diggers   lifting the ground
up   putting it back down   sequences
of high-rises   morsels of nervous
collectivity   isolated dreams
in stacked childhood bedrooms
teenagers on swings

on pills   carcinogenic pieces
of daily living   the embers of
hearth-life

Shame and I
had never greeted one another
before today   but we've known
each other intimately since our infancy
I don't have a single cell left
in common with that earlier iteration
and since then   the plain mention of *trauma*
has become cliché   our
accidentally-unoriginal core
life experiences and their solutions
made peripheral   as if rearranging air
When glass is clear enough   you can't even tell
the façade exists   all those shards
somehow held together   One day
it has to crack

Just because you can see out of the window
doesn't mean you are outside
Isn't that a Shame
in itself

PART THREE EDGE

ANIMAL CRUELTY

spring character couldn't tell

how played-with felt like love   but
secret   arousal became a song

kept inside   animals

hurt and die every second
some survive   hurt

becomes just part of our
                                        road

tell the lamb inside you
they're safe

,

,

;

& ,

,

;

.

memory is just punctuation

TO PLEASE HIM,

I told him
I wanted to be just like him
when I grew up. Instead
of grin, he cringed.
I was never sure if
he'd winced at the lie
or the
tragedy of such a suggestion;
his sun too much
to stare at, nonetheless
there all the time.
The non-
essential self was perceived
through fathers'
unmet needs—
our flawed human
instinct to reason
We are the same, therefore I
surely
won't burn

AT BAY

No swimming amidst the archipelago today, jellyfish are lethal today, a barrier at the coast constructed between Tunisia and Sicily. No one on Grindr 'round here has a face; I take myself searing through siesta, lose my bearings entirely in an onion field, catch sunstroke. That night, unmanned, I return to the shore for a soak in residue of my estranged heritage—to reflect, of course.

~

The last time I saw him was when I confronted him in person. A therapist had suggested it might be something worth doing, or not. I chose to go through with it in the light hours of a dwindling rave, flying from anaesthetics and revenge fantasy. That I was *on drugs* soon became his defence, I heard; but it was a consequence. An outcome of action minus accountability is chaos. This was also when I came out to him. The two shouldn't have been connected in my head.

~

A way to fall asleep is to visualise you're drowning and accept it; I wriggle deeper in the solution to where it's too darkened to see. There's a nip at my vertebrae. I giggle, a threat reflex, and choke on the discreet salt of my genealogy, ectoplasm for a sunken gaze. Surfacing, I touch my soft spine. The sting isn't that bad. I laugh at it, at the memory. There's humour in the darkness—after a while, your eyes just get used to it.

~

The last time I saw him

I was

drowning

and

Surfacing

~

WHERE WE CONNECT

the long neck of afternoon
the multitudes
which surround & differentiate
nothingness & the unknown
are all that we miss
we kiss
with all the passion
of a service station
& autoimmunocentric calculations
his jaw like he chews on
the stale ends of a loaf
with forced lips
he thought he was gaining me
but he was losing me
i'm feeling unreal
from the impulse for absence of ache
& thinking about something else
the beyondness of the universe
resembling a womb
the floating in-between
every meeting with you
is a meeting about our lives
i don't know anything
only aware of the
saliva in my mouth
the goods
from a pub toilet vending machine
approaching a delible rush
the ringing horn
of bagpipes cuts through the flat

that has an air of homosexual loneliness
oh
oh
man
to perform masculinity
requires an audience
so i'm almost myself in the dark
he compliments what's visible
they like it when i don't eat properly
if remembering touch is subjective
then what is muscle memory?
sped to reflection
braced for the future
a body reenacts the world
the unresolved
returning in flesh
as the turquoise sea is largely unexplored
so too is a brain
when i last had my fingers inside you
they were dyed that flaming colour
this seems less profound to me today
thinking of my lover
while on my back for another
i've decided fucking is not imperative
to my individual liberation
but as a smidgen of universal sexual rights
when fire engulfs
& settles to ash
supposing that i never want
to reach a peak again
never lasts long
we fuck to be inserted with better things
for a second depth
a delusion of freedom
in the human zoo

it's not as reductive
as gay guys going nuts
an anal cleft symbolises perseverance
of the years i've yearned to participate
in this erotic theatre
as though my life depended on it
& it did
i leave his place in the rain
wet rot of nature's breath
i delete the app
i redownload the app
kill me
when my last load hits the floor

( )

God sends me a photograph of myself. That's me, they say. I say *I am the real me, not you.* They say: you are not me, *I am me,* I mean, I am you.

PERFORMANCE ARCHIVE

In Athens, I'm hunched in front of stone
reliefs of ancient nude warriors,
fantasising about you. Some are faceless,

cockless, just the balls and calves
remain. Others, their wreck
of limbs held in imagined positions

with plastic rods, which, en masse,
gives a pleasant illusion
of patriarchal dismantling. Imagine.

Some of their noses are, like my own,
battered; a bust representing a goddess
bears what appear to be tears

staining the marble train from one eye
due to chance oxidisation, we're told.
The women statues are described as young

and owned. All are perceived
as white due to modern display,
an uncolouring.

This preservation of big, bald heads
and erotic fragments. It's funny
proclaiming them men and women

when they were just chiselled.
The fantasies we insist on,

and those I keep to myself

among the rubble that's left
as rubble, and that which is
propped up for effect.

AFRAID OF FRICTION

I was due to be writing a novel; everyone I admired was doing it. I made a start by typing down *I am fascinated by hybridity,* and returned my senses to real life, pressed to notice myself in the pluriverse of the city street.

As I turn a corner into the shade, an expensive-looking man walks towards me, wearing a T-shirt with the word HYBRID written across the chest, and a bright silver car pulls up behind him: a Hybrid. I descend some stairs into the station, no fixed destination in mind.

The hybridity of a person has long been used to brutalise them, yet variance is the truest human tone. I'm drawn to phrase myself in a way which is uncategorisable, to be genrequeer. Call it obfuscation, or a disempowered disinterest for rules—to proceed in spite of formality.

Hurtling underground in a tin can, I stall in the normative state of noticing. Can I savour my life, or just be writing about it? I increasingly don't think in sentences, why do I translate into them? Continuously composing in an attempt to keep living, the line that could lead this way or that; the long poem of the years, completing themselves.

A cohesive narration cannot be manufactured of life, as life is not cohesive, whereas arc arises regardless of wilful plotting; time is a loop, equator to our work-in-progress of being—the evolving bounds of your compound form.

That being said, my fiction is overwritten by the many ellipses of dissociation, and when my novel ended, it was barely a page long.

What is my fucking purpose?

To make a somewhat poetic
gesture when all that surrounds
it is reality?

DUTY OF CARE

the origin of love is a delirium
and it persists   love
        you were beside me
        when i thought i'd had enough

        you know me
        better than binary   devotional sight
                of accepting one another's change
                our infatuations with others
                        you inevitably make
                        beautiful sense to me

love   i'd kiss the muck into your forehead
        in our uneventful happiness   you let me
                forget about the worst   thank you
                for erasing a part of me
        i couldn't stop reading over

                        & love   once all is done with
                the remaining specks of us
                will remember that we did exist
                        a pair

THE *I* FUNCTION: AN ERASURE

Set Oedipus free, join the monsters, do not hide patriarchal violence
behind the so-called incestuous desire of children . . .
I ardently appeal for . . . the mutation of psychoanalysis
Paul B. Preciado

Conception sheds the I,
illuminative intelligence indeed. Useless
gestures reflect the child's own body,
jubilant little identification.
Transformation takes place,
a form prior to being objectified.
Ego maturation a mirage
in symmetry that reverses appearance:
hallucination, or homeomorphic desire.
Social structures limit reality.

In dreams, aggression appears
in the form of growing wings, a
camp metaphor for free
experiential condition. Language
would remain a symbolic reduction.
Repression decisively tips being
human into an abstract awareness of
latencies; even in the pretense of society,
freedom is affirmed within the walls
of self-perception. Neurosis provides us reform

—the ecstatic cipher of our journey.*

* Words erased chronologically from 'The Mirror Stage as Formative of the *I* Function as Revealed in Psychoanalytic Experience' by Jacques Lacan

OH, EMPTINESS

All speech is failed music
Jameson Fitzpatrick

I pace around outside the entrance
of a building site, smoking, as he exits
his body on a strategically overstrained NHS
ward, from the same act's lingering, cell-
altering effects. I admit the bleak irony
in reprising a stage of loss determined by
what you choose, also,
to keep doing. The fantasy of choosing
what's done inside you
by your own hand, mortal,
dimming, like a match lit for no reason
but habit. As if it could connect us
across planes now. Later,
hovering
in the bath I've taken to
spoiling myself in, I notice
how my hastening heart rate
sends reverberations, a rhythm, out
of the scaffolding of itself and through
the water, shifting inanimate
detritus, and wonder
if this throbbing could still
move you
as we perform
the act of erosion
in harmony.

I have been walking through reverberations with no sense of what the event was

Nuar Alsadir

Do I not have a plot to my life?

Clarice Lispector

how far can you run from your past?

the world is only

so big

EPILOGUE MIRROR

The thrashing sky blends into an apparently-still sea
made of the same thing   My stretched-out blood
vessels reveal sixty-thousand miles of nerves
and the potential for transmission   symbiosis
of traveller   earth and path   Pilgrimage
is ever relational

All the while   God sends me a chain
of question marks   followed by
Waste of time   I agree
the disembodied
lines of topographic borders
aren't real   nor the concept of self
nor God

Anyway   my battery dies

That at the time I couldn't understand it   is different to
misremembering   When I understood is when I broke down
Break down language enough   the lyric you buried rises back up

The bus stalls in flooding   breaking down and needn't be fixed
I realise I've been ignoring the rain the whole time   The road
has turned into a pond   as the land will eventually give in to sea

Sooner or later   you have to just stop   When a dark sheet
is thrown on you   you can chuck it back   A life's rhythm
emanates from periods of light and lack thereof   begging the
versatility to change route when necessary   We choose to cut
out the poison or let it thrive

Exiting the bus like it's the past   as both begin to sink   the driver
asks *What's your addiction?*   *Identity*   I answer   and vomit on
the current ground   frothing-over from withdrawal

Shame wakes   always after—   and I'm elsewhere   alone with
the surface of the road   until only the road remains   my shadow
left behind   When Shame is handed down to you   it is not
yours   Perhaps a new life can be simply walked to   Transition
nor recovery are destinations

An ending is an ending   often you don't even notice you've
been brought to it   just spaces between one thing and the next
Surely verging on something novel

We are always returning   a queer deviation
from straight lines   There is a vividness in being
moved between two points   something existing
far away and then   miraculously   up close   The end
has already happened   Will happen again

The horizon is foregrounded
by illegible vibrancy   the resounding voice of
I can change   All the conflicting layers
between flesh and reflection
compose the wandering parts of a life

And why is life worth living?
the psychiatrist asks me again   this time
in my subconscious   *To decide to live*
freely   I imagine saying   To know
you are worthy of life
Don't waste your freedom
in this place   he might have said back

There's more to life than riding
on pity   in the future there are survivors
This truth opens out in front of me
like a hot mouth

The death of Shame can still feel
like a loss   I could take it
with me anywhere

I got out   I   I   I
             I   I   I

think it was enough

To be healed we must be dismembered, pulled apart.
The healing occurs in disintegration
Gloria E. Anzaldúa

For just a moment
I'm not at all occupied by where I'm going
Mícheál McCann

How I got here: gravity
Bhanu Kapil

GRATITUDES

Sincere thanks are given to everyone who read *Limbic* and supported it so generously.

'Oh, Emptiness' includes epigraphs from 'That Goddess' by Sharon Olds, *A Queen In Bucks County* by Kay Gabriel and 'Address' by Jameson Fitzpatrick.

'Prologue' includes epigraphs from *Queer Phenomenology: Orientations, Objects, Others* by Sara Ahmed, *To* After That (*Toaf*) by Renee Gladman, *Time Is the Thing a Body Moves Through* by T Fleischmann and 'Accident Report in the Tall, Tall Weeds' by Ada Limón.

'Pseudomorph' is titled from the glorious work of Sabrina Imbler and includes an epigraph from their essay 'My Metamorphosis'.

'Afraid of Friction' references the concept of pluriversality, which I first encountered in *Constructing the Pluriverse: The Geopolitics of Knowledge* edited by Bernd Reiter.

'The *I* Function: An Erasure' includes an epigraph from *Can the Monster Speak?: A Report to an Academy of Psychanalysts* by Paul B. Preciado, translated by Frank Wynne, and is composed of words erased chronologically from 'The Mirror Stage as Formative of the *I* Function as Revealed in Psychoanalytic Experience' from *Écrits* by Jacques Lacan, translated by Bruce Fink.

'Epilogue' includes epigraphs from *Fourth Person Singular* by Nuar Alsadir, *Água Viva* by Clarice Lispector, translated by Stefan Tobler; *Light in the Dark/Luz en lo Oscuro: Rewriting Identity, Spirituality, Reality* by Gloria E. Anzaldúa, edited by AnaLouise Keating; 'Just After Rain, 6 p.m.' by Mícheál McCann and *The Vertical Interrogation of Strangers* by Bhanu Kapil.

These citations are included with gratitude and admiration for the writers, their work, and the ideas that they have inspired. Thank you for your influence.

Many thanks are due to the generous editors of the journals, anthologies and media outlets in which extracts from this book have previously appeared: *The North, Z9Magazine, berlin lit, fourteen poems, Books Up Close, PROTOTYPE, Seaford Review, You're Never Too Much, Counselling Matters, Queerphoria* and *bath magg*. In memory of Gboyega.

Thank you to Homotopia Festival and A Lovely Word for commissioning the first performance of poems from this book, in Liverpool – thanks also to Queer Bodies Poetry Collective for their involvement and support. Thanks to Ledbury Poetry Festival for hosting me and facilitating valuable dialogue. Thank you to Vlad, Alex and Z9Festival for organising my visit to Sibiu, and Crina for translating from this book into Romanian. Thanks to Burley Fisher Books, QUEERCIRCLE and the Psychology department at University of Westminster for their support and commissioning workshops based on elements of this book.

'Oh, Emptiness (1)' is for Keith M. 'Refractal' is for David P-C. 'Imodium' is for Adam. 'For the Buzz' is for Ellie and for Glasgow. 'Oh, Emptiness (2)' is for Keith J. 'Animal Cruelty' is for Day. 'Afraid of Friction' is for Oluwaseun. 'Duty of Care' is for Conor. 'The *I* Function: An Erasure' is for So.

For being readers, advisers, friends; thank you to Adam, Aimee, Alice, Amy, Andrew, Avery, Ben, Bernie, Bethany, Brendan, Chris, Darryl, David M, David P-C, Day, Dermot, Ellie, Gary, Harry M, Harry P, Isabel, Jack P, Jack Y, Jamie, Jessica, Jim, Julia, Katie, Keith J, Keith M, Kostya, Mí, Misha, Lewis, Liam S, Nisha, Olivia, Oluwaseun, Piero, Robbie, Rosalie, Rich, Sam, Selali, So, Stephanie, Stephen, Tash, Tom, Troy. In memory of Azusa.

Thanks to Anna for Anzaldúa. Thanks to Ewan for Alsadir.

Thanks to L for ending *Loners*.

Thank you to Ruby and Jess for their time, feedback and encouragement. Thanks to all the advance readers for this.

Thank you to the NHS workers for their care in 2022, and always, under ridiculous organisational strain. Thanks to Kevin (for the title) and Jerry (for the clarity).

Thanks to the Keappock-De Ceapóg-Roes, for their love and enthusiasm. Thank you to Irisini for TM. In memory of Vincent.

For the readers and booksellers, thank you all.

To Jack and Ellis, what a pleasure it's been to do this again! Thank you so much for encouraging and believing in the writing. Here's to round two!

Thanks also to Oliver, Wolf and Liam K (and Sid!). Thanks to Laura for the typesetting magic.

Thank you to Nicasio for his inspiration, belief and conversations, and permission to use his beautiful painting for the cover.

Thank you to my agent Martha for her perceptiveness and insight, advocacy, and generosity.

Thank you to my mum for all her support.

To Conor, for carrying us through.